Cyber Citizenship and Cyber Safety™

Privacy and
Hacking

Tamra Orr

Mater Dei Catholic High School
1615 Mater Dei Drive
Chula Vista, CA 91913

rosen publishing's
rosen central®

New York

Published in 2008 by The Rosen Publishing Group, Inc.
29 East 21st Street, New York, NY 10010

Library of Congress Cataloging-in-Publication Data

Orr, Tamra.
Privacy and hacking: cyber citizenship and cyber safety / Tamra Orr.—
1st ed.
    p. cm.
Includes bibliographical references.
ISBN-13: 978-1-4042-1352-4 (library binding)
1. Computers and children. 2. Computer hackers. 3. Internet—Safety measures. I. Title.
QA76.9.C659O77 2008
372.6—dc22

                                                        2007033800

Manufactured in Malaysia

Contents

Introduction

Welcome to the World of Hacking

HACKERS FIND A WAY
TO WIN GIVEAWAY CARS!

COMPUTER PHREAK USES A CEREAL WHISTLE
TO MAKE FREE INTERNATIONAL CALLS

CYBERCRIMINAL ALMOST GETS AWAY WITH
20,000 STOLEN CREDIT CARD NUMBERS

COMPUTER WORM "MELISSA" WREAKS
HAVOC FOR MILLIONS

MICROSOFT SHUT DOWN FOR DAYS
BY HACKERS

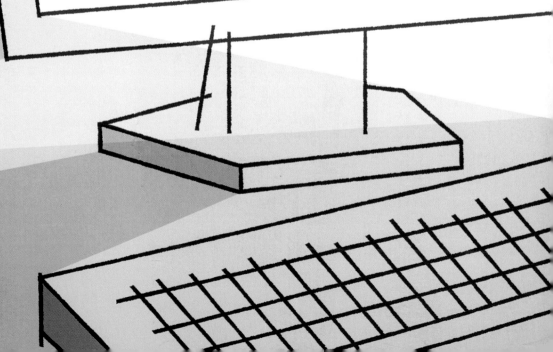

Do the headlines on the facing page sound overly dramatic? Each one is based on a true story! The world of computer privacy and hacking is a busy one—and creates everything from mild amusement to complete catastrophe.

What image pops into your head when you hear the word "hacker"? If you were asked this question twenty years ago, most likely you would struggle to come up with any answer at all. Today, the word is used frequently and often inaccurately.

Before anyone can understand the term "hacker," it is important to understand how computers changed the world. Although they have been around for almost half a century now, they were not familiar to most people until the late 1970s and early 1980s. Today, sixty-two million homes in this country have at least one computer. Just a few decades ago, however, they were found only in large businesses and hectic places like banks, airports, and police stations. They took up a great deal of room and worked slowly. The Internet was still just something that only the biggest computer experts knew about.

As the Internet has grown, thrived, and really exploded, so have its problems. One of the biggest issues is security. With so much important and top-secret information flying about the wireless world, it was not long before some people realized that by stealing this data, they could make a lot of money. Following hot on their heels were companies and software designers doing their best to protect that same

Famous Crackers

John Draper, aka Cap'n Crunch: He found a whistle in a cereal box that made the same sound as AT&T's long-distance switching system. He used it to make free long-distance calls all over the world (before cell phones) and showed others how to do it, too.

The 414 Gang: In nine days, this gang broke into more than sixty computers, including some at Los Alamos National Laboratory, which helps develop nuclear weapons.

Robert T. Morris Jr.: He was a graduate student who launched a computer worm—the Morris worm—spread to six thousand computers.

Kevin Paulson: Paulson and his friends rigged a radio station's phone system to allow only their calls when contests were held, thus winning two Porsches, several vacations, and $20,000 before getting caught.

Kevin Mitnick: A celebrity in the world of hacking, he stole more than twenty thousand credit card numbers before getting caught.

Jonathan James: Only sixteen years old, he cracked computers at the Department of Defense and NASA, claiming that he "was just looking around, playing around."

information. Some hired specially trained personnel to explore every corner of their online programs and find and repair any vulnerable spots. These people were actually referred to as "hackers." They were the good guys! On the other hand, the "bad guys" were the "crackers," who snuck in as thieves. They were just as knowledgeable, dedicated, and skillful, but they had one main difference. They were there to steal, not protect.

Just before he drove from San Francisco to Lompoc, California, on October 26, 1976, to start serving his four-month prison sentence, John Draper took the time to give a quick interview. His crime was defrauding the Pacific Telephone Company by making free long-distance calls.

When you think of important information on the Net that could be stolen, you may think of Social Security numbers, government secrets, military data, or even details about terrorists. While those examples are good ones, there is other information that you may have overlooked that can lead to trouble. It could be your address and telephone number. It could be your locker

Part of Kevin Mitnick's punishment for hacking was promising to stay far away from any device that could help him break into corporate or university computers.

combination or savings account number. All of these are private numbers that could result in a real mess if they became public, thanks to some sneaky cracker.

Let's take a look at hacking and how it helps and hurts us. Once you see how vulnerable you can be, you will want to be a lot more careful about what you do—and do not do—when you go surfing on the Web.

Chapter 1

Perks with a Price

There is no doubt that computers have drastically changed the world in countless ways. They are available 24/7 in a way no other system has ever been before. Banks, stores, libraries, schools, and government offices all shut down at some point during the day. People stop answering phones, opening mail, taking orders, and performing services, but computers are still ready to perform every single hour of the day, every day of the year. They never take a day off or go on vacation.

At work, computers have made jobs faster and safer, as well as more efficient and precise. They cut down on paperwork. They keep lines of communication open. They help with everything from accounting to inventory. At home, families can do their banking and bill paying online. Students can have up-to-date research at their fingertips. You can plan

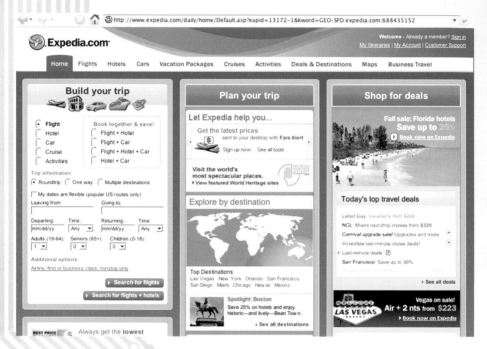

Booking an entire vacation—renting a car, getting a plane ticket, and making hotel reservations—takes only a few clicks on sites like Expedia.com.

trips, read articles, watch videos, and buy and sell anything imaginable. Computers allow people to communicate instantly—no more waiting for someone to answer the phone, read a letter, or meet you somewhere. Teachers can instantly respond to a student's questions. People can apply for jobs, car loans, and even mortgages and know in seconds if they are eligible. Check the weather for your town or any other town on the entire planet. Scan movie times. Check the stock market. Buy or trade stocks. Compare car prices.

Beyond Working

Of course, computers are about more than research and work. You can play countless types of games with people in your community, in the neighboring state, or somewhere on the other side of the world. Download free music. E-mail or send an instant message to a friend. Join a chat room. Read a blog or create your own. Post your stories, poems, songs, or artwork. Print your photos.

Computers have changed the way we speak. Not long ago, terms like "dot-com," "reboot," "download," and "spyware" would have meant nothing at all. Now we tend to toss them around as easily as we talk about cell phones and other high-tech gadgets.

Paying the Price

There is no doubt that computers have changed lifestyles for the better, but as mentioned before, those perks have not come without a price. As we continue to pour all of this information onto the Web—not just our numbers and statistics, but our personal information as well—we risk it spreading out to people who may be criminals or predators, or just someone who doesn't care about our privacy. After all, as culture changes, so does its crime. When people go digital, crime goes digital, too. When this happens, the computer can become less of an incredible invention and more of a potential danger.

Using credit cards to make purchases online may be the ultimate in convenience, but it can also carry a high price if too much personal—and financial—information is put on the Net.

The world on the Web is simply not the same world as we live in on a daily basis. It operates on a different level of rules and ethics. You would not walk up to a person at the bus stop and start chatting and, within a few minutes, divulge your banking information. You wouldn't turn to the person behind you in line at the grocery store and spout off your address and phone number without serious thought. You aren't going to walk into the middle of a restaurant and start handing out your usernames and passwords to whoever is in the room. You are not going to stop by a coffeehouse and blatantly flirt with every person sitting there, regardless of age, intent, appearance, or background. Yet, many people do these very things when they go online. They fill out order forms with their banking information. They share where they can be located with their "new friends." They share secret passwords because "hey, we are buddies." Worst of all, they flirt with people who are "safe" because they are the same age, have the same interests, and live miles away—maybe. It's easy to think that your private information is going to stay private, but with today's incredibly determined hackers and focused predators, and a Web that keeps going and going like the Energizer Bunny on espresso, you may well be wrong.

Hackers are smart. Crackers are brilliant. They are like private detectives determined to find out the most secret, most personal information about you that they can and then find a way to use it. They get a rush from the hunt and a thrill from the catch. Make sure you aren't the bait. Learn to stay out of the net when you are on the Net.

Chapter 2

Inside Cyber Criminals

While you are online looking up a fact for your science report, checking headlines on your favorite news sites, updating your blog, or hanging out with friends in some of your favorite chat rooms, there are people who may be keeping a close eye on you. These predators are watching and waiting for the chance to take advantage of innocent surfers, often young ones who are willing to accept people for who they say they are. Sadly, the personas some put forth on the computer have nothing to do with who they really are. They may be a different age and gender, with far different interests and motivations from what you think. It is sobering to realize that almost one in five young Internet users receive unwanted sexual solicitations. The vast majority of these solicitations occur when a child is on a home computer. Just as you have

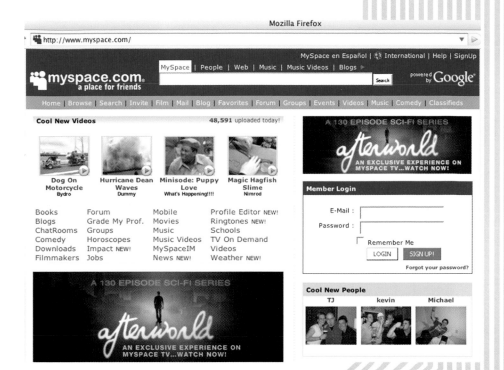

MySpace is one site people use to write about their lives and meet new friends. Unfortunately, some "friends" may not be who they say they are.

been told not to believe everything you read, it is essential that you not believe everything you are told online.

In North Carolina, for example, a middle-aged man told a thirteen-year-old girl who he was talking to online that he was seventeen. He asked her where she lived and, unfortunately, she told him. He showed up at her house, pretending to be the seventeen-year-old's dad. To get closer to the girl, he started dating her mother. This went on for months until the girl realized that her "online boyfriend" and his "dad" were actually the same person. She continued to chat with him, however, and even agreed to run away with him. Fortunately, he was arrested when a female police officer posed as the girl and he came to pick her up. Officers found tape and rope inside his truck.

Other Cyber Criminals

Sexual predators are only one kind of cyber criminal today. While this type manipulates the computer in order to meet and lure in victims, other computer criminals are much more interested in manipulating data. Many of them are computer experts who really enjoy using their skills to either obtain private information off the Web so they can use it or to send something destructive out into the Internet, like a worm or virus. Some are motivated by nothing more than simple curiosity, while others might be inspired by revenge or anger. Some cyber criminals want the feeling of power that comes with disrupting the lives of others, and some just want to see what they are personally capable of doing. Crimes range from the trivial to the traumatic. Can they wipe out a personal traffic ticket—or the tickets of everyone in the state? Can they change a grade or change the name on a credit card account? Can they hack into a school's test scores or into a bank's savings accounts? Can they crash the computer of someone they don't like or the computers of the whole city?

Criminal Categories

Marcus Rogers, associate professor at Purdue University in West Lafayette, Indiana, is in charge of the university's cyber forensics research. He divides most computer criminals into seven categories:

- **Novice:** Limited abilities, usually just looking for attention
- **Cyberpunk:** Can write own software, tends toward credit card number theft
- **Internal:** Unhappy employee/ex-employee/petty thief motivated by greed
- **Coder:** Has hidden agenda, often mentors newbies, motivated by power
- **Old guard hacker:** Likes using brain to create havoc, usually not criminal
- **Professional criminal:** "Gun for hire," well trained, state-of-the-art equipment
- **Information warrior/cyber terrorist:** Well funded, usually political

Hollywood Stereotypes

For years, Hollywood has perpetuated the idea that hackers are lonely computer geeks with huge brains and nonexistent social lives. They are usually portrayed as spending all day and

Shhhhh! Keeping Secrets

Do not reveal:

1. Your last name
2. The full names of anyone in your family
3. Your home address
4. Your phone numbers
5. Your screen name, user ID or password
6. Any kind of banking information
7. Your Social Security number

Take the time to:

1. Look at a Web site's privacy policy to see how it uses the information you provide. In April 2000, the Federal Trade Commission (FTC) set up new rules for Web site operators in order to help protect young people's privacy online. If the site collects any kind of personal information about kids, they have to have a privacy policy posted somewhere. This policy must list:

   • Type of personal information collected (name, address, e-mail, and hobbies)
   • How the site will use this information
   • Whether personal information is forwarded to advertisers or third parties
   • A contact at the site

   Find the policy and read it. Share it with your parents, too. Then, together you can decide if you want to give consent or not. Also keep in mind that you can take back your consent at any time and your information will be deleted. To find out more, contact the FTC at 1-877-FTC-HELP.

2. Talk to your parents about the sites you visit. Have them look at the sites, too.
3. Leave a site if it makes you uncomfortable or asks for more information than you are willing to share.
4. Stick to Web sites recommended by your school and family.
5. Try using a pseudonym (a fake name) when online.
6. Tell your parents immediately if someone online is urging you to meet him or her face to face.
7. Remember that just because a person gives you facts about him/herself, not a single one is necessarily true, including age, location, gender, interests, and hobbies.
8. Never ever forget one rule: if you put the information online, you run the risk of it becoming known. Whether it's your latest crush, your current weight, your future dreams, or just a comment about someone, if you go online with it, it is no longer private. If you want it kept private, keep it offline.

night sitting in front of their screens doing amazingly intricate and complicated things but are unable to carry on a simple conversation with people in real life. While once that image might have been somewhat true, today's hacker is quite often charming and very social. It is part of what he or she needs to do in order to obtain the information he or she needs.

The 1983 movie *War Games* starred Matthew Broderick as a teenager who accidentally, when trying to play a video war game, taps into the nation's defense system and almost starts a nuclear war. This movie was many people's first introduction

War Games, a 1983 movie starring Ally Sheedy and Matthew Broderick, was an eye-opening film for some watchers, as suddenly the public realized that computers were far from foolproof.

to the idea that computers were vulnerable. At that time, they were just thought to be huge, complicated, and rather mysterious machines that everyone was raving about. Most people had no concept that computers might also be potentially dangerous. Today, that picture is completely different, as most people know that the many advantages of a computer come with some serious threats as well. While it is terribly unlikely that you could trigger World War III, not being careful while you are online could trigger problems in your own life—so take precautions.

Chapter 3

Hacking: A Right or a Crime?

Is hacking necessarily a bad thing? It sounds like a simple question, but it is an important one to think about. While most people would definitely say yes, there are other opinions out there.

For example, Emmanuel Goldstein, editor in chief of *2600: The Hacker Quarterly*, says, "Hacking is, very simply, asking a lot of questions and refusing to stop asking. This is why computers are perfect for inquisitive people—they don't tell you to shut up when you keep asking questions or inputting commands over and over again. But hacking doesn't have to confine itself to computers." He adds, "Anyone with an inquisitive mind, a sense of adventure, and strong beliefs in free speech and the right to know most definitely has a bit of the hacker spirit in them." Goldstein believes that today's

Proving that nothing is really safe from determined computer hackers, in 1997, signs in the New York subway read "The Hacker Quarterly" and "Volume Fourteen, Number Three" instead of the usual "Have a great day" and "Watch your step."

hackers are like yesterday's explorers—excited by the search and what they may find. Although he certainly does not condone using hacking for anything illegal or destructive, he also believes that hackers are a necessary part of life. As he puts it, "People have always been attracted to adventure and exploration. Never before have you been able to get this without leaving your house and without regard to your skin color, religion, sex, or even the sound of your voice. On the Internet, everyone is an equal until they prove themselves to be a moron. And even then, you can always start over. It's the ability to go anywhere, talk to anyone, and not reveal your personal information unless you choose to—or don't know enough not to—that most attracts people to the hacker culture, which is slowly becoming the Internet culture."

On the other hand, Dr. Charles Palmer, manager of Network Security and Cryptography and head of the Global

Security Analysis Lab, disagrees. "Hacking is a felony in the United States and most other countries," he says. "Some of the 'joyriders'—hackers who access systems just for the challenge—think it's harmless since they usually don't 'do' anything besides go in and look around. But if a stranger came into your house, looked through everything, touched several items, and left (after building a small, out-of-the-way door to be sure he could easily enter again), would you consider that harmless?" he asks. "These joyriders could be causing damage inadvertently since just by their presence they are using system resources."

For the people who are wild about the Internet and cannot imagine doing anything more fun than exploring it for hours in hopes of finding back doors, trap doors, loopholes, and other cracks to slide into, hacking is not only a pleasure, it is a right. They equate it to being an astronaut out in space or a mountain man looking for a trail from one snowy top to another. What might be right around the next star or peak? Many of them are also driven by curiosity to learn more about the world of the Web and then use it to design new software. Certainly most of them are "white hatters," there only to learn and explore, not to do harm. Here is how one hacker described the experience:

Hackers are the elite corps of computer designers and pro-grammers. They like to see themselves as the wizards and warriors of tech. Designing software and inventing algorithms

Safe Sites

With so many sites out there potentially leading to trouble, where can you go and trust that you are fairly safe? Here are a few suggestions:

www.ala.org/greatsites
This Web site from the American Library Association is a great source for trustworthy and helpful Web sites.

www.timeforkids.com
This Web site is a companion to *Time for Kids* magazine and has everything from interesting news stories to games and research help.

www.congressforkids.net
Need help with a government question? Check this site out.

www.askforkids.com
Formerly "Ask Jeeves," this is a great Web site to get some of your questions answered.

www.bookdivas.com
This site is for young adult and college readers who want to learn about new books and talk to others who have read the same titles.

www.cybersleuth-kids.com
A reliable Internet search guide for grades K through 12.

http://encarta.msn.com/encnet/departments/homework
Encarta's Web site for kids is for those who need help with homework assignments.

can involve bravura intellection, and tinkering with them is
as much fun as fiddling with engines. Hackers have their own
culture, their own language. And in the off-hours, they can
turn their ingenuity to sparring with enemies on the Nets, or
to the midnight stroll through systems you should not be able
to enter, were you not so very clever . . . It's a high-stress life,
but it can be amazing fun. Imagine being paid—well paid—
to play forever with the toys you love. Imagine!

Others, however, may disagree and feel that hacking, just
by virtue of what it is—accessing computers without the
owner's permission—is wrong, even a crime. As Palmer says,
they may equate it with a person coming into your house
without your permission or knowledge and looking around.
Even though he or she may not steal or damage anything, is
even the person's mere presence acceptable to you? While
some people might say yes, many would say an absolute no.
The idea of sneaking into other people's computers and
other company's networks may sound thrilling from the
hacking end, but from the other side, it can feel invasive,
threatening, and infuriating—even if the hacker just came by
to show that it was possible and then went away.

Hackers get on the Net for many reasons, most of them
fairly harmless. After all, when Steven Wozniak and Steve
Jobs created the first truly successful commercial computer,
they did it by hacking the systems that they could find and
learning from them. The vast majority of the people working

Many hackers are just trying to learn more about computers. That is how Apple's Steve Jobs, John Sculley, and Steve Wozniak, pictured here in 1984, got their start.

to crack a security code are not those malevolent "black hatters" or bad guys who want to find out where you live, how to steal your money, or crash your computer. They are simply curious explorers who want to know more and are willing to use your system to do it. Is that OK?

The jury is still out.

Computer Crime
and Punishment

E xactly how far does cyber crime go? Who does it affect and how can it be punished? The following stories are a good glimpse into those answers.

In 2002, Joseph McElroy, a British sixteen-year-old, wanted to hack into a powerful network so that he could download and store movies and music from the Internet. It was a goal that he shared with countless other teens across the globe. However, McElroy had better computer skills than some, and in the process of connecting to this stronger network, he developed software that gave him access to a top-secret U.S. research center. Along with other hackers, he accessed the system located at the Fermi National Accelerator Laboratory, and it began to slow down. When technicians realized they were being hacked, they panicked. They were

Gary McKinnon is shown here in May 2006. He was charged with perpetrating the "biggest military computer hack of all time."

sure a terrorist attack was imminent, and the computers were shut down for three days. The U.S. Department of Energy sounded a full-scale alert. The breach was quickly traced to McElroy's house, and he was arrested. The alert resulted in more than $50,000 in damages and expenses—and a lot of fear.

There is little as startling as checking your e-mail and being told you have a bounty on your head, but that is just what happened to a man named Peter McGlothin. The e-mailer told McGlothin that someone had put out a contract on McGlothin's life, but if he sent the hit man $30,000, he would not fulfill that contract. Despite warnings to stay away from the police, McGlothin called them and found that his was only one of many complaints about this same scam.

A fifteen-year-old named Amy had wanted Internet service at home for a long time. In the meantime, she accessed the Net from the library and school. She met "Bill" in an online chat room, and he sympathized with her about parents who didn't seem to understand what kids needed. When Amy did not come home from school one day, her mom immediately

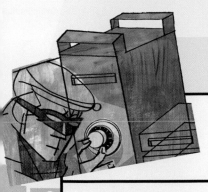

What Does Cyber Crime Cost?

According to the FBI, cyber crimes cost us a lot more than just worry. They cost the country a lot of money.

- Cost to U.S. businesses to deal with viruses, spyware, PC theft, and other computer-related crimes: $67.2 billion per year
- The average cost per company: $24,000
- Amount spent responding to worms and viruses: $12 million
- Amount spent on theft: $3.2 million
- Amount spent on financial fraud: $2.8 million
- Amount spent on network intrusions: $2.7 million
- Companies reporting one to four computer threats/virus infections in 2005: 51.5 percent
- Companies reporting five to nine computer threats/virus infections in 2005: 20.1 percent
- Companies reporting ten to nineteen computer threats/virus infections in 2005: 9.1 percent
- Companies reporting twenty or more computer threats/virus infections in 2005: 19.2 percent

knew something was wrong. She found a note in her daughter's room mentioning taking a bus to meet up with Bill. She contacted the police and they tracked her daughter down, but the incident didn't end there. Three weeks later, the man came to Amy's house, and she went with him to a nearby hotel, where she was assaulted. She also found out that Bill had been meeting girls like this for some time. Although Amy came home safe, Bill is now behind bars for kidnapping another fifteen-year-old.

Jerad Rose of Louisville, Kentucky, decided to buy some computer equipment online. It was simple. He used his debit card and it took only a few minutes. Three days later, however, while looking at his online bank statement, he noticed an unauthorized purchase for $825. Quickly he went to his bank and canceled his card. It was too late. By then, more than $1,600 had been charged to his account, overdrawing it. He had to spend hours on the phone calling merchants, canceling credit cards, and reporting the incident to the Internet fraud department of his bank.

Hundreds of business owners throughout the United States and Canada suddenly found out that the Better Business Bureau had filed a complaint against them—or maybe not. "Phishers" sent out these e-mails under the guise of the Better Business Bureau—one of the most trusted names in the country. The e-mails attempted to elicit private information about the companies. The BBB immediately sent out a warning that these messages were not coming from it and to report the fake e-mails to the authorities.

Prison Time

Cyber crimes are all over, and they are expanding into new areas, requiring new vigilance, new laws, and new punishments.

Hackers work on computers at the 2002 H2K2 conference in New York City. There, security professionals and computer activists develop new techniques and software.

In the past, many cyber criminals were treated with not much more than a slap on the hand and a warning. Should hackers get prison sentences? Are their crimes as severe as those of other criminals? Should the teenage hacker trying to change his grade on a math final get the same sentence as one who hacks into the Pentagon? These are tough questions that people involved in justice have to think about and discuss. Is prison the right response to computer crimes? How about paying back money lost or community hours? Is that enough?

In recent years, the U.S. Sentencing Commission has grappled with all of these questions. In late 2003, they began imposing stiffer penalties. Hackers who stole personal data were given a 25 percent longer jail sentence. If the data was then sold to a third party, the sentence was even longer. Break-ins to online accounts are punishable based on the amount of money in the account, not the amount stolen. Virus authors saw their sentences increase by 50 percent.

According to John G. Malcolm, deputy assistant attorney general and head of the U.S. Justice Department's computer crimes section, "The increases in penalties are a reflection of the fact that these offenses are not just fun and games; that there are real world consequences for potentially devastating computer hacking and virus cases."

In December 2004, Brian Salcedo, one of three men who hacked into the national computer system of Lowe's hardware stores to steal customers' credit card numbers, was sentenced to nine years in prison. One of the prosecutors stated, "I think the massive amount of potential loss that these defendants could have imposed was astounding, so that's what caused us to seek a substantial sentence against Mr. Salcedo."

Will tougher sentences make a difference? Law enforcement officers think so, but Kevin Mitnick, one of the world's most well-known hackers, doesn't see it that way. "The person who's carrying out the act doesn't think about the consequences and certainly doesn't think they're going to get caught," he says. "I really can't see people researching what the penalties are before they do something."

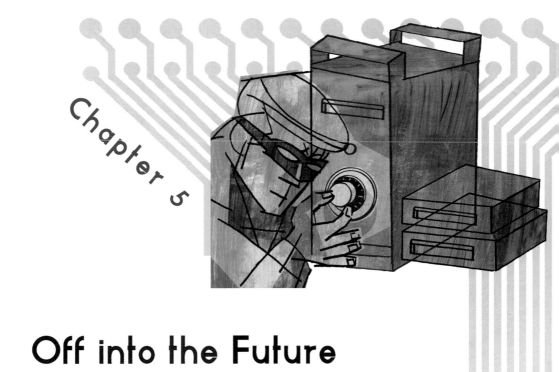

Chapter 5

Off into the Future

What does the future hold for both hackers and those who fight hard to stop them?

Already a number of protections are in place and are constantly being updated and improved. Firewalls, antivirus software, and antispyware are repeatedly being modified to cope with the avalanche of worms and viruses attacking the Net on a daily basis. Law enforcement agencies at the local, regional, and national levels are being trained in how to meet the growing demand for computer security at home and at work. Justice departments, judges, and lawyers are learning about computer crimes and how to cope with them. Education on how to stay safe online and awareness of online dangers are keys to making a difference. As Dr. Charles

Myths and Facts

Myth: All hackers are out to get you.

Fact: Actually, hackers are often the talented and helpful "white hatters" who prevent cyber crime from happening in the first place. Companies and individuals occasionally hire these skilled workers to find problems in their security systems and repair them. These "ethical hackers," as they are labeled, go into computer systems and networks and find the potential weak spots. Then, they find a way to close, repair, or strengthen them. It is the "cracker" who has maliciousness on his or her mind. However, that word is rarely used, and "hacker" has come, in today's society, to mean the computer criminal.

Myth: Cyber criminals are loners who spend all their time on the computer instead of with people.

Fact: That image is one that Hollywood and others have stereo typed. It may have once been somewhat accurate but not any longer. The serious hacker who is looking to create havoc is frequently one that has multiple social skills and charm in order to achieve the trouble he or she is attempting.

Myth: Hackers rarely get punished for their   computer crimes.

Fact: In the beginning, there was truth to this, simply because the justice system had no idea what to do with these criminals. Cyber crimes were all new, and new punishments and laws had to be developed in order to know what to do when a person was arrested and convicted of one. However, in recent years, penalties for hacking have continued to get tougher, and some people are in prison for five years or more because of these crimes.

Palmer puts it, "As long as there are unsecured computers with interesting stuff on them, there will be hackers."

Another step in improving computer security is the smart card, also known as the chip card or formally as the integrated circuit card. Smart cards act like electronic wallets, with the ability to act as debit cards, fuel cards, credit cards, and identification. They would be very difficult to hack in any way.

No matter what kind of protection is designed, however, it is likely that hackers will keep right on cracking them. It is in their blood. As Emmanuel Goldstein says, "As long as the human spirit is alive, there will always be hackers. We may have a hell of a fight on our hands if we continue to be

As computer viruses continue to attack computers around the world, many companies have fought back by making better virus protection software.

imprisoned and victimized for exploring, but that will do anything but stop us."

Staying Safe Online

With all of those cyber criminals out there just hoping to find someone to take advantage of, you need to take action. How can you keep your computer—and all it knows about you—safe? Take this advice, straight from the big guys at the FBI.

1. Keep your firewall turned on. This is the software that helps prevent your computer from those who might be trying to get in and crash it, delete your data, or just sneak off with your passwords.
2. Install and/or update antivirus software. This software will protect your computer from other software that someone might want to embed in it. It looks for malicious code and if it finds it, attacks it, and removes it as fast as possible.
3. Install and/or update antispyware technology. Spyware is appropriately named. It spies on you when you are online to track your habits, especially your spending ones. Other people watch what you are doing. Make sure your computer has antispyware on it—but be careful which one you buy. Some of them are actually spyware in disguise. Sneaky, eh?

4. Keep your operating system up to date. Your software needs to be periodically updated to make sure it has the latest information out there for fighting those nasty viruses and worms. You need the newest medicine to battle these illnesses.

5. Be careful what you download. Never open an e-mail attachment from someone you do not know, and be wary of attachments even from those you do. They may contain malicious coding. Also get permission from your parents before downloading anything from the Net to your computer.

6. Turn off your computer. Although many people tend to leave their computers on 24/7, this just increases the number of hours the machines are vulnerable. Turn yours off while you are gone at school, going to bed, and so on.

Taking It Personally

While the antivirus companies work on their end, it is essential that computer users like you do your part as well. Learning the dangers of the Net is a good first step. Then, take action. Pay close attention to the tips and ideas here and follow them. Remember that the Net is a great place but not necessarily a safe place. Be careful what you put on the Net and who you talk to while you're there. Use all the software you can to filter out viruses and worms. Last, take time to become a good "cyber citizen" yourself. How? Here are some tips.

- Respect the privacy of others.
- Never try to break into another computer. It's not a game—it's a crime.
- Don't steal copyrighted computer programs by copying them off the Net.
- Don't download any copyrighted books, magazines, or music without permission from their creator.

Computers really are the best thing to come along since, perhaps, the printing press. They make everyone's lives more fun, educational, entertaining, and full, but there is often a price to pay for it all. Make sure you do all you can to enjoy the perks safely and legally.

Glossary

antispyware Software that protects from spyware, which secretly gathers user information through a user's Internet connection, usually for advertising purposes.

antivirus software Software that has been designed to protect a computer from viruses and other threats.

back door A hole deliberately left in place in a computer's security system so that service technicians can get in to maintain it.

blog An online journal.

chat room An online place where a group of people can all talk together.

crackers Mischievous—even malevolent—hackers.

firewall A network security barrier that guards the entrance to a private network or computer.

hackers Computer experts who study systems in order to improve them.

instant messaging A type of immediate communication on the Web.

phishing Using fake versions of bank Web sites to grab login details of customers.

phreaking Originally referred to as the science of cracking the telephone network and now sometimes used to refer to any kind of security cracking.

sexual solicitation Attempt to lure a person into having sex.

virus Dangerous computer program that is usually able to make copies of itself in order to spread.

wizard A person who has specialized knowledge about certain software or hardware.

worm A self-replicating computer program, much like a virus, but it does not need to be a part of another program in order to spread.

For More Information

CyberAngels
P.O. Box 3171
Allentown, PA 18106
Web site: http://www.cyberangels.org
 An organization that provides Internet safety information to
 schools and families, as well as works to stamp out computer fraud.

CyberTip
Canadian Centre for Child Protection
615 Academy Road
Winnipeg, MB R3G 0N4
Canada
Web site: http://www.cybertip.ca
 Canadian organization that works to inform and protect children
 from online danger.

Family Online Safety Institute Offices
666 Eleventh Street NW, Suite 1100
Washington, DC 20001
Web site: http://www.fosi.org
 Organization dedicated to keeping families informed about dangers
 on the Internet.

Net Smartz
123 N. Pitt Street, 3rd Floor
Alexandria, VA 22314
Web site: http://www.netsmartz.org
  An organization that provides children and teens with tips on how
  to stay safe online.

Web Sites

Due to the changing nature of Internet links, Rosen Publishing
has developed an online list of Web sites related to the subject
of this book. This site is updated regularly. Please use this link
to access the list:

http://www.rosenlinks.com/cccs/prha

For Further Reading

Adams, Simon. *Code Breakers: From Hieroglyphs to Hackers.* Minneapolis, MN: Tandem Library, 2003.

Knittel, John, and Michael Soto. *Everything You Need to Know About the Dangers of Computer Hacking.* New York, NY: Rosen Publishing, 2002.

MacDonald, Joan Vos. *Cybersafety: Surfing Safely Online.* Berkeley Heights, NJ: Enslow Publishers, 2001.

Marshall, Elizabeth. *Student Guide to the Internet.* Wallingford, CT: Millbrook Press, 2000.

Rothman, Kevin. *Coping with Dangers on the Internet: A Teen's Guide to Staying Safe Online.* New York, NY: Rosen Publishing, 2000.

Sherman, Josepha. *The History of the Internet.* London, England: Franklin Watts, 2003.

Verton, Dan. *The Hacker Diaries: Confessions of Teenage Hackers.* New York, NY: McGraw-Hill Osborne Media, 2002.

Weber, Michael. *Invasion of Privacy! Big Brother and the Company Hackers.* Boston, MA: Course Technology, 2003.

Bibliography

BBC News. "A-Z: Hack Attack." February 11, 2000. Retrieved June 8, 2007 (http://news.bbc.co.uk/1/hi/uk/639248.stm).

BBC News. "Cyber Criminals Step up the Pace." December 6, 2004. Retrieved June 9, 2007 (http://news.bbc.co.uk/1/hi/technology/4072647.stm).

Beaver, Kevin, and Stuart McClure. *Hacking for Dummies.* Indianapolis, IN: For Dummies, 2006.

Bednarz, Ann. "Profiling Cybercriminals: A Promising but Immature Science." Network World. November 29, 2004. Retrieved June 8, 2007 (http://www.networkworld.com/supp/2004/cybercrime/112904profile.html).

Black, Jane. "Cybercrime Victims Hit Back—Online." *Business Week.* October 10, 2002. Retrieved June 5, 2007 (http://www.businessweek.com/technology/content/oct2002/tc20021010_3368.htm).

Business Week. "Meet the Hackers." May 29, 2006. Retrieved June 4, 2007 (http://www.businessweek.com/magazine/content/06_22/b3986093.htm).

Evers, Joris. "Computer Crime Costs $67 Billion, FBI Says." C/Net News.com. January 20, 2006. Retrieved June 10, 2007 (http://www.news.com/2102-7349_3-6028946.html?tag+st.util.print).

Fairfax Digital. "Teen Hacker Triggered Nuclear Terrorism Alert." February 4, 2004. Retrieved June 4, 2007 (http://www.smh.com.au/articles/2004/02/03/1075776065349.html).

Information Database: The Cyberpunk Project. "Hackers." December 7, 2004. Retrieved June 3, 2007 (http://project.cyberpunk.ru/idb/hackers.html).

Insurgency on the Net. "Two Views of Hacking." Retrieved June 8, 2007 (http://www.cnn.com/TECH/specials/hackers/qandas).

IT Security. "Top 10 Most Famous Hackers of All Time." April 24, 2007. Retrieved June 6, 2007 (http://www.itsecurity.com/features/top-10-famous-hackers-042407/).

Kendall, Sandy. "Teen Hacker or Cybercriminal: How Do We Draw the Line?" CSO. December 1, 2003. Retrieved June 5, 2007 (http://www.csoonline.com/talkback/120103.html).

Krebs, Brian. "Cyber-Criminals and Their Tools Getting Bolder, More Sophisticated." *Washington Post*. March 14, 2007. Retrieved June 5, 2007 (http://www.washingtonpost.com/wp-dyn/content/article/2007/03/13/AR2007031301522.html).

Mitnick, Kevin, and William Simon. *The Art of Intrusion: The Real Stories Behind the Exploits of Hackers, Intruders and Deceivers*. Indianapolis, IN: Wiley Publications, 2005.

PCWorld.com staff. "Timeline: A 40-Year History of Hacking." November 19, 2001. Retrieved June 6, 2007 (http://archives.cnn.com/2001/TECH/internet/11/19/hack.history.idg).

Shanbhag, Raju. "Cybercriminals Rely on Mind Games to Scam Internet Users." TMCNet. June 25, 2007. Retrieved June 30, 2007 (http://internetcommunications.tmcnet.com/topics/enterprise/articles/7909-cybercriminals-rely-mind-games-scam-internet-users.htm).

Think Quest. "Cybercrime: Piercing the Darkness." Retrieved June 10, 2007 (http://library.thinkquest.org/04oct/00460/future.html#crimeCriminals).

USA Today. "Lowe's Hardware Hacker Gets Nine Years." December 15, 2004. Retrieved June 12, 2007 (http://www.usatoday.com/tech/news/computersecurity/hacking/2004-12-15-lowes-hack_x.htm).

Index

About the Author

Tamra Orr is a full-time author living in the Pacific Northwest. She has a degree in English and education from Ball State University. She spends most of her time sitting in front of a computer writing (not hacking!). She is the author of almost 100 nonfiction books for kids of all ages, and she writes for more than a dozen national educational testing companies. She is a mother of four (ages twenty-three, sixteen, fourteen, and eleven) and a wife to Joseph. When she isn't writing or researching, Orr is reading something intriguing, watching the sunset on the nearby mountains, or hanging out with her family. During the course of writing this book, she stopped three times to check her antivirus software.

Photo Credits

Cover Les Kanturek; p. 7 © AP Photos; pp. 8, 28, 36 © Getty Images; p. 12 © Alan Schein Photography/Corbis; p. 20 © MGM/courtesy Everett Collection; pp. 22, 26 © AP Photos; p. 31 © Reuters/Corbis.

Designer: Les Kanturek; **Editor:** Beth Bryan
Photo Researcher: Marty Levick